Countries Around the World
Japan

Patrick Catel

www.raintreepublishers.co.uk
Visit our website to find out more information about Raintree books.

To order:
☎ Phone 0845 6044371
📄 Fax +44 (0) 1865 312263
🖥 Email myorders@raintreepublishers.co.uk

Customers from outside the UK please telephone +44 1865 312262

Raintree is an imprint of Capstone Global Library Limited, a company incorporated in England and Wales having its registered office at 7 Pilgrim Street, London, EC4V 6LB – Registered company number: 6695582

Text © Capstone Global Library Limited 2012
First published in hardback in 2012
Paperback edition first published in 2013
The moral rights of the proprietor have been asserted.

Edited by Abby Colich and Claire Throp
Designed by Ryan Frieson and Steven Mead
Original illustrations © Capstone Global Library Ltd, 2012
Illustrated by Oxford Designers & Illustrators
Picture research by Ruth Blair
Originated by Capstone Global Library Ltd
Printed and bound in China by CTPS

ISBN 978 1 406 23548 7 (hardback)
15 14 13 12 11
10 9 8 7 6 5 4 3 2 1

ISBN 978 1 406 23555 5 (paperback)
16 15 14 13 12
10 9 8 7 6 5 4 3 2 1

British Library Cataloguing in Publication Data
Catel, Patrick.
Japan. -- (Countries around the world)
952'.05-dc22
A full catalogue record for this book is available from the British Library.

Acknowledgements
We would like to thank the following for permission to reproduce photographs: Corbis pp. 6 (© Carmen Redondo), 8 (© Asian Art & Archaeology, Inc.), 11 (© issei kato/Reuters), 13 (© Koichi Kamoshida/ZUMA Press), 16 (© George Steinmetz), 24 (© Bloomimage); Dreamstime.com pp. 14 (© Retina2020), 21 (© Rinusbaak), 39 (© Image Focus); Getty Images pp. 10 (Keystone), 15 (Jeremy Maude), 25 (Toshifumi Kitamura/AFP), 31 (Nicolas Asfouri/AFP); iStockphoto pp. 18 (© Prill Med\[ien\]design & Fotografie), 32 (© inci aral), 35 (© efesan); Shutterstock pp. 5 (© omers), 19 (© redswept), 20 (© Smileus), 23 (© Galina Barskaya), 26 (© Thomas Nord), 28 (© Thomas La Mela), 30 (© testing), 33 (© bonchan), 37 (© Radu Razvan), 46 (© Christophe Testi).

Cover photograph of Mount Fuji, Japan reproduced with permission of Corbis (© David Ball).

We would like to thank J. Philip Gabriel and Mika J. Perry for their invaluable help in the preparation of this book.

Every effort has been made to contact copyright holders of any material reproduced in this book. Any omissions will be rectified in subsequent printings if notice is given to the publisher.

Disclaimer
All the Internet addresses (URLs) given in this book were valid at the time of going to press. However, due to the dynamic nature of the Internet, some addresses may have changed, or sites may have changed or ceased to exist since publication. While the author and publisher regret any inconvenience this may cause readers, no responsibility for any such changes can be accepted by either the author or the publisher.

Contents

Some words in the book are in bold, **like this**. You can find out what they mean by looking in the glossary.

Introducing Japan

What do you picture when you think of Japan? Is it amazing bullet trains and the neon lights of Tokyo? Or perhaps you picture sushi and karaoke? The ancient island nation of Japan is all of those things, but it is also much more.

Japan is made up of hundreds of islands, but has four main, large islands: Hokkaido, Honshu, Shikoku, and Kyushu. This land of the mighty **samurai** and snow-capped Mount Fuji is used to challenges, both man-made and natural.

Japan faced its greatest test yet when the most powerful earthquake in its recorded history struck off the east coast, near Sendai, on 11 March 2011. The earthquake triggered a devastating **tsunami**, which is a giant ocean wave that can come up far on to land. The earthquake and tsunami caused thousands of deaths and billions of pounds in damage.

Road to recovery

The disaster created another major concern when the Fukushima Daiichi nuclear power plant was damaged. International teams fought bravely to prevent a major disaster and the spread of harmful **radiation**. Japan knows about the harmful effects of nuclear radiation. It is the only country in history to have suffered the attack of a nuclear bomb, at Hiroshima and Nagasaki, before its defeat in World War II (1939–1945).

Since World War II, Japan has worked to become the third-largest **industrial** power of the world, and a nation known for cutting-edge technologies. It has kept its ancient, unique sense of **culture** and honour, even while becoming a modern nation.

How to say...

In Japan you might hear *konnichiwa* when welcomed, which means "hello" or "good afternoon". The Japanese say *moshi moshi* as "hello" when using the telephone.

Japan is known for its colourful, neon, night-time cityscapes.

History: from shoguns to peaceful democracy

People have lived in Japan since around 30,000 BC in the Stone Age. This was during a time when prehistoric humans made tools from stone and hunted and gathered food. Around 10,000 BC the people of Japan developed the Jomon **culture**. *Jomon* means "cord pattern", and these people were named after the cord patterns found on their pottery.

The Horyu Temple in Nara is the oldest Buddhist temple in Japan. Buddhism arrived in Japan from China in the mid-AD 500s and influenced Japanese culture.

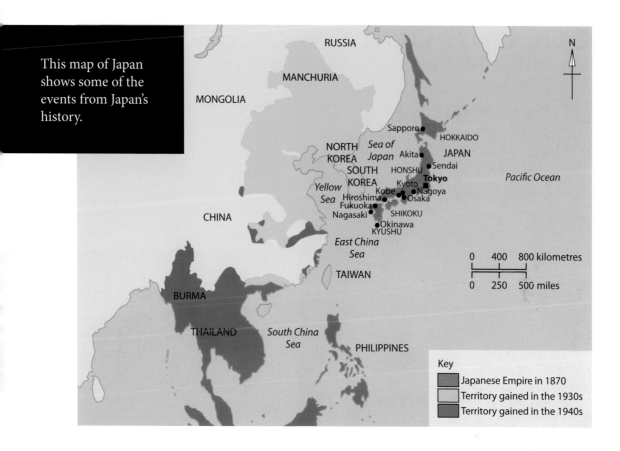

This map of Japan shows some of the events from Japan's history.

According to legend, Japan was founded by Jimmu, the first **emperor**, in 660 BC. Around 250 BC a wave of people from mainland Asia, called the Yayoi, took over the Jomon culture to become the dominant culture in Japan. They brought farming and metalworking with them. The Yayoi also followed a new religion, which eventually developed into **Shintoism**.

The emperor and Asian influences

In the AD 500s, the Yamato **clan** controlled Japan. It began the **imperial dynasty** that has ruled in Japan ever since.

At the same time, Chinese ideas and styles came to Japan and influenced its culture and new government. These Chinese ideas and styles included **Buddhism**, **Confucianism**, writing, art, **architecture**, and dress.

Samurai and shoguns

Beginning in the 1100s, Japanese warriors called **samurai** took power in Japan. They were trained in martial arts, sword fighting, and archery (bows and arrows). If a samurai lost his honour or brought shame to his clan or leader, or if he needed to avoid capture, he took his own life in a ritual called *seppuku*. *Seppuku* involved plunging a short blade into the abdomen (stomach).

In 1185, Minamoto Yoritomo, head of the Minamoto clan, established a new government. He was given the title of **shogun,** or chief military commander, in 1192. There was still an emperor, but the real power now lay in the hands of shoguns. They helped rule Japan for 700 years, with samurai working loyally for them.

The samurai were skilled swordsmen.

New arrivals

Rival shoguns and clans fought each other in wars that lasted until the late 1500s. Then, in 1543, a Portuguese ship blew off course and was wrecked near Japan's southern shore. Japanese shoguns were amazed at Portuguese firearms. They began trading for them, usually offering precious metals in exchange. Other European traders soon followed, along with people spreading **Christianity**.

Isolation

In 1639, fearing invasion, the shoguns closed Japan to outside influence and drove out all foreigners. Japan remained closed off from the outside world for about 200 years. Only a handful of Dutch traders were allowed to live on an artificial island in Nagasaki harbour called Dejima. During this time, the city of Edo (now Tokyo) was the centre of government. By the 1700s, Edo had a population of more than one million people. It was larger than any other city in the world at the time.

Modernization

Japan's isolation ended in 1853, when US Commodore Matthew Perry arrived with a fleet of ships. Japan was no match for the military technology of the **West**, and it was forced to accept foreign trade and influence.

In 1868, the young Japanese emperor Mutsuhito established a new government and began to make Japan more modern. This period is called the Meiji Restoration. The age of the shoguns was over.

Japanese empire

Japan quickly improved its **industry** and military. Japan then fought wars with China and Russia, adding parts of their land to its territory. By 1915, Japan was the most powerful nation in Asia. Japan's military began to take greater control in the country's government. In 1937, it attacked deep into China, in search of more territory.

World War II (1939–1945)

The United States tried to stop Japan from these attempts to expand. At first, the United States used **sanctions**. On 7 December 1941, Japan responded with a surprise attack on the US Navy's Pacific Fleet at Pearl Harbor, Hawaii. The United States then entered World War II. They joined the **Allied forces**, who had been fighting Germany since 1939.

After a hard-fought war in the Pacific, the United States dropped atomic bombs on the Japanese cities of Hiroshima and Nagasaki in August 1945.

Hirohito (on the right) was emperor of Japan during World War II. Here he walks through an area of Tokyo damaged by US bombs.

At least 150,000 people died at the time of the bombings. Many more died later as a result of exposure to the **radiation** from the bombs. Japan surrendered a few days after the second atomic bomb.

Japan today

Japan was officially occupied by the United States until 1952. The Occupation government established a new **constitution** based on US ideals of **democracy**. In the last decades of the 1900s, Japan became a great, peaceful, **industrial** nation. Today, it is known for its technology and its strong **economy**. Many items you use today, such as video games and portable music devices, were invented in Japan.

Disaster

On 11 March 2011, a massive earthquake occurred on the northeast coast of Japan. A

Japan's current emperor is Akihito, who succeeded his father, Hirohito, in 1989. He is shown here with his wife, Empress Michiko, at their daughter's wedding.

tsunami followed. Thousands of people died. Half a million Japanese people lost their homes. Damage to a nuclear power plant, as a result of the natural disaster, added to the worries of the Japanese people as radiation affected food and drinking water in the surrounding areas. The government suggests 25 trillion yen (£189 billion) will be needed to rebuild after the disaster.

Regions and resources: a nation of islands

Japan is a chain of islands located on what is known as the Ring of Fire. This is a zone along the edge of the Pacific Ocean that suffers from frequent volcanoes and earthquakes due to the movements of the earth's plates. Undersea earthquakes can cause **tsunamis**.

How to say...

Some Japanese place names contain directions. *Kita* means "north", *minami* means "south", *higashi* means "east", and *nishi* means "west". The Kitami Mountains, for example, are found in northern Japan.

Mountains run along Japan's four main islands like a spine.

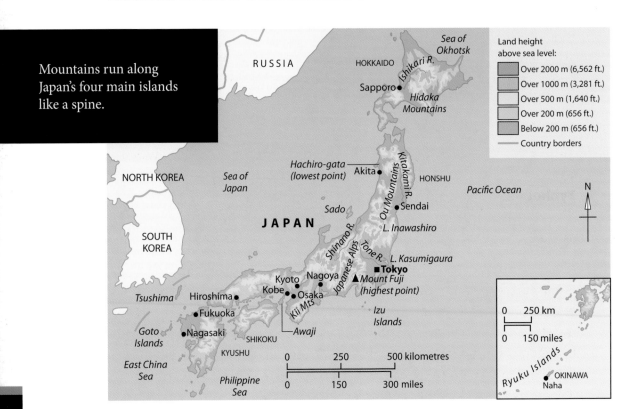

Japan suffered a devastating earthquake in 2011.

Natural disasters

In 2011, Japan faced its worst earthquake in recorded history off the east coast of Honshu. The US Geological Survey called it the Tohoku earthquake. A devastating tsunami followed, wiping out entire towns and killing thousands. Japan's worst recent earthquake before this was in Kobe in 1995, which killed 6,400 people. A severe earthquake in Tokyo in 1923 killed about 140,000.

Climate

Japan's climate is generally warm and humid in summer and cold in winter, with heavy snows on the west coast and island of Hokkaido in the north. **Typhoons** and flooding sometimes occur in the summer.

The land

Mountains and hills cover more than 80 per cent of Japan. Mount Fuji, a volcano, is Japan's highest peak at 3,776 metres (12,388 feet). It has not erupted since 1707. Most of Japan's plains are along the coast, where rivers meet the sea. The capital city, Tokyo, is located on the Kanto Plain, Japan's largest lowland, on the island of Honshu. Japan has many short rivers. Only the Shinano and Tone are more than 310 kilometres (200 miles) long. The Shinano is Japan's longest river. Japan has few lakes.

Cities

Japan's major cities are located on its plains. Tokyo is the capital and largest city, with over 13 million people. Japan's cities are growing and merging together into an area called the Tokaido Megalopolis. This is a belt of cities about 483 kilometres (300 miles) long, stretching from Tokyo to Kobe, along the southeast coast of Honshu. It includes Tokyo, Kawasaki, Yokohama, Nagoya, Osaka, Kobe, and Kyoto. The Tokaido Megalopolis is the Japanese centre of business, **industry**, higher education, and international trade.

Agriculture

Only 13.2 per cent of Japan's land is farmed. About 7 per cent of the population is made up of farmers, and many of them also work other jobs. Most farms are small (about 1.4 hectares, or 3.5 acres). Rice is by far the most farmed crop. It is grown on more than half of the farmed areas in Japan.

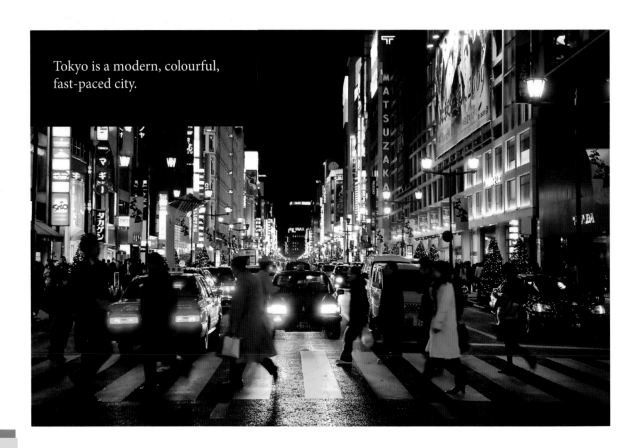

Tokyo is a modern, colourful, fast-paced city.

Tsukiji, at Tokyo Bay, is the world's largest fish market.

Other Japanese crops include wheat, barley, potatoes, sugar beets, and vegetables. Mandarin oranges are a major fruit crop, and Japanese meat production has grown over the last decades. Many farm areas specialize in crops such as tea, tobacco, or hops.

Resources

Japan has few mineral resources, but the waters all around Japan are a great resource. Seafood is a large part of the Japanese diet, and Japan is one of the world's leading fishing nations. Its yearly catch is more than 7.5 million tonnes, which is estimated to be worth more than £8.5 billion. Japan also farms seafood and seaweed, which account for a part of the Japanese diet.

Japan's products are traded around the world. This is a Honda plant in Suzuka, Japan.

Import partners (2009)

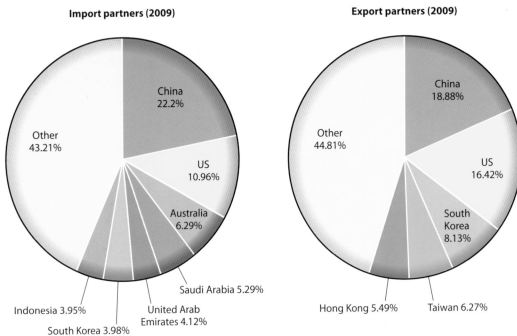

China 22.2%

US 10.96%

Australia 6.29%

Saudi Arabia 5.29%

United Arab Emirates 4.12%

South Korea 3.98%

Indonesia 3.95%

Other 43.21%

Export partners (2009)

China 18.88%

US 16.42%

South Korea 8.13%

Taiwan 6.27%

Hong Kong 5.49%

Other 44.81%

Japan's greatest trading partners are China and the United States.

Industry

By the end of the 1900s, Japanese brand names – including Sony, Panasonic, Toshiba, Toyota, Honda, Nissan, Mitsubishi, Mazda, Canon, Hitachi, and Nintendo – were well known around the world. Japanese electronics and automobiles are **exported** worldwide and have built a reputation for reliability, value, and cutting-edge technology. Those industries have helped Japan maintain one of the largest **economies** in the world.

Japanese work culture

The Japanese deeply value company and family ties. Hard work and loyalty are highly valued in Japanese **culture**. Bosses are respected in the same way as parents, and employees are seen as family. Until recently, most workers stayed with one company until they retired at the age of 60. That has changed somewhat since Japan struggled economically in the 1990s, and young workers now change jobs more frequently.

YOUNG PEOPLE

The jobless rate for young people in Japan has been high in recent years. Many Japanese companies recruit workers who are still in university. Some companies do not accept applications from people who have already graduated from university. In 2010, the new minister of Japanese Health, Labour, and Welfare requested that companies consider applications from people up to three years after they graduate from university.

Wildlife: cranes, chrysanthemums, and more

Throughout their history, the Japanese have shown a respect for nature. Japan has a variety of plants and animals to match its varied climates. Forests cover most of the land that has not been cleared by humans.

Sub-tropical plants such as palms and **bamboo** grow as far north as central Honshu. **Rainforests** exist on the southernmost islands of Japan. There are a few **mangrove swamps** on the southern coast of Kyushu.

Animals

Japan has a variety of animals. Japan's forested mountains are home to animals such as bears, wild boars, foxes, deer, antelope, hares, monkeys, and raccoon dogs. The raccoon dog resembles a raccoon, with dark facial markings and a yellowish-brown coat.

The Japanese word for the raccoon dog is *tanuki*.

Japanese macaques are large, shaggy-haired monkeys with pink faces and short, furry tails. They are important figures in Japanese myths and folktales. Many live in Jigokudani Monkey Park, which is part of the Joshinetsu Kogen National Park. It is located in mountains near the centre of Japan. Japan has 29 national parks that work to preserve its natural wonders.

Water life

There are many fish **species**, as well as whales and porpoises, in the seas around Japan. Colourful carp found in Japan's rivers and lakes are also kept as pets called *koi*, which are kept in garden ponds.

Japanese macaques, or snow monkeys, warm themselves in hot springs, where steam and hot water bubble up from underground.

Hanami parties are held in the spring to view the cherry blossoms.

Reptiles, amphibians, and birds

Japan also has many varieties of turtle, lizard, and snake. The Japanese giant salamander can grow to over 1.2 metres (4 feet) long. Japan has about 150 species of songbird, as well as many other types of bird. Many water birds, including herons, ducks, swans, and cranes, live in Japan for at least part of the year.

Plants

The chrysanthemum flower is honoured in Japan as a symbol of the **emperor**. Cherry trees are planted throughout Japan and are important in Japanese **culture**. In the spring, television news includes reports on the best places to see cherry trees bloom. The beautiful cherry blossoms don't last long. In **Buddhism**, the blossoms symbolize the temporary nature of life.

Environmental issues

Japan's development of **industries** has had a negative effect on the **environment**. Animals such as the Japanese crested ibis and the eastern white stork have died out.

Japan took steps after 1970 to improve its air and water quality. Today, however, Japan suffers from **acid rain** due to air **pollution** from mainland Asia. Japan itself continues to face worldwide pressure to stop its practice of whaling (hunting whales).

YOUNG PEOPLE

The Japan Youth Ecology League, or Eco-League, was founded in 1994. Its members and management are young people between the ages of 16 and 29. The purpose of the Eco-League is to encourage young people to work for a better environment. The group hosts gatherings, promotes environmental education, and helps students who are looking for jobs related to protecting the environment.

The red-crowned crane is a rare, large crane with a patch of red skin on its head.

Infrastructure: a constitutional monarchy

Japan's current **constitution** became law on 3 May 1947. Based on text prepared by **Allied forces** after World War II, the constitution built upon an earlier constitution from 1889. According to the new constitution, a parliament was created and all adults 20 years old and over could vote. Women were given the right to vote for the first time. The **emperor** became a symbol of the state and unity of the people. It became a ceremonial, **hereditary** role without real power. Akihito has been emperor since 7 January 1989.

Government

Japanese citizens vote for members of the Japanese parliament, called the Diet, which is the legislative (law-making) body. The Diet has two houses.

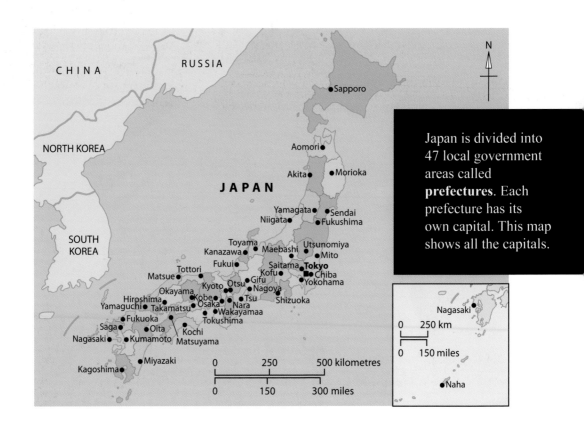

Japan is divided into 47 local government areas called **prefectures**. Each prefecture has its own capital. This map shows all the capitals.

Tokyo is Japan's capital and centre of government.

The House of Councillors, or Sangi-in, has 242 members who are elected for six-year terms. The House of Representatives, or Shugi-in, includes 480 members who are elected for four-year terms.

The prime minister is the head of Japan's government. The Diet decides who becomes prime minister. After elections, the leader of the majority party in the House of Representatives usually becomes prime minister. The prime minister appoints a cabinet to help run the executive branch. Naoto Kan has been prime minister since 8 June 2010.

The Supreme Court heads the judicial branch, with justices appointed by the cabinet. A chief justice is appointed by the emperor, after approval by the cabinet.

Education

The Japanese consider education the best way to achieve success and fulfillment in life. In order to get into the best schools, pupils work very hard, beginning at a young age. The good schools bring higher social status and the ability to get the best job after graduation. Schools are very competitive. There are many high-pressure tests to take throughout a Japanese pupil's school career. Pupils' futures and school choices are decided by tests as early as primary school.

Most Japanese pupils wear uniforms to school.

YOUNG PEOPLE

Most schools in Japan require uniforms. As in Japanese homes, pupils take off their street shoes when they arrive at school and wear slippers or indoor shoes in the classroom. Pupils are often expected to help clean their classrooms after school. They also clean during school, such as after lunch before they go on their break. After that, many pupils go to private "cram schools", called *juku*, for two to three hours in order to prepare for exams. Some children have lessons on Saturdays for even more instruction.

These Japanese students are participating in a **calligraphy** writing contest.

Japanese children begin nursery school at about three years old. They begin primary school at the age of six, and then middle school at the age of twelve. After middle school, pupils attend secondary school, where most take courses to prepare for university. Some pupils take technical classes to prepare for a career. Japanese **culture** and education traditionally encourage being part of the group. However, today's Japanese society increasingly values creativity and **individualism**.

Transportation

Japan's transportation system is one of the most modern in the world. People can travel quickly between cities using one of Japan's bullet trains. Japan has several airports with international service and flights between Japanese cities. Most Japanese people live in cities and travel to work or school by train or subway. Most city streets are crowded with cars, bicycles, and people, with terrible traffic jams during rush hour.

Daily life

Japan is about the same size as Germany. Its population is the tenth largest in the world. It can be a very crowded place! People living in the cities get used to small flats and crowded trains. Tokyo underground trains are so crowded that *oshiya*, or "people pushers", work to squeeze people tightly onto a train so the doors can close!

Japanese bullet trains travel at more than 290 kilometres (180 miles) per hour.

Health care

Japan has one of the best health care systems in the world. National health insurance covers all Japanese citizens. The **life expectancy** for people in Japan is 82.17 years, which ranks as the fifth highest in the world. At the same time, fewer babies have recently been born in Japan. As a result, the average age of the population is getting older.

The Japanese consume fewer calories and less fat than Europeans and Americans, eating more seafood and vegetables. However, more Japanese people are overweight now, as foods from the **West**, such as red meat and dairy, have become more readily available.

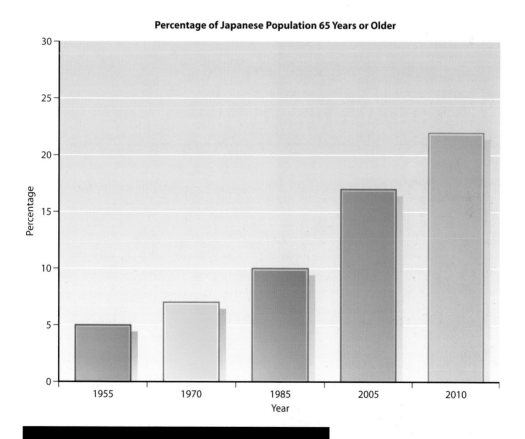

Percentage of Japanese Population 65 Years or Older

Japan is experiencing an ageing population that requires government support.

Culture: proud traditions and modern expressions

Japan is proud of both its ancient traditions and its modern success. The combination of ancient and modern gives Japan a unique and fascinating **culture**.

Japanese geisha dress in **kimonos**.

Ancient traditions

Many ancient Japanese traditions are still popular today. The arts of **calligraphy** (artistic writing), flower arranging (called *ikebana*), gardening, and the tea ceremony are popular, especially with Japanese women. The poetic form of **haiku** also continues to be popular in Japan.

Japanese geisha are now rarer than they once were. Geisha are women trained in the arts of dancing, singing, and providing entertainment.

Japanese performing arts are influenced by the country's history. Japan has several forms of traditional theatre. The Noh play combines music, words, and dance. The Bunraku is a puppet play that combines music, words, and dancing. Men in colourful costumes perform in Kabuki plays, which have singing, dancing, and even special effects.

Religion

Shintoism is a religion unique to Japan, with **shrines** all around the country. It includes historical Japanese figures and natural objects among its many gods and spirits. Many Japanese people combine Shinto traditions with **Buddhism**, which was introduced from Korea and China. The Chinese philosophy of **Confucianism** also influenced Japanese culture. **Christianity** has a small following in Japan.

Daily life

In the traditional Japanese home, floors are covered with woven straw mats called *tatami*. *Fusuma*, which are sliding doors covered in paper, are used to separate rooms. People take off their shoes in the entrance area inside the home. Japanese people sometimes eat sitting on floor cushions, called *zabuton*, at a low table. At night, mattresses called *futons* are unrolled onto the floor for sleeping, although more city families and young people now use beds.

Ethnic groups in Japan

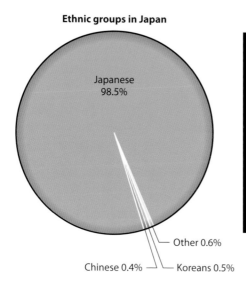

Japanese 98.5%

Other 0.6%

Chinese 0.4% — Koreans 0.5%

Most of the minority population of Japan is Chinese or Korean. A small group of Ainu people in Hokkaido has preserved its cultural identity. They were badly treated by the Japanese, who discriminated against them and took over most of their land. In 2008, however, the Japanese finally recognized the Ainu as native people.

Holidays and festivals

The New Year, or Shogatsu, is Japan's biggest celebration of the year. Families clean their homes and shops at the end of the year to prepare to celebrate New Year. On New Years Day families gather to eat a traditional feast. The birthday of the **emperor** is also always a national holiday.

Coming of Age Day celebrates 20-year-olds becoming adults. Greenery Day is 4 May and is part of Golden Week, when people travel to the countryside or abroad. Among other holidays is one for boys and girls called Children's Day. (See page 38 for a full list of holidays.)

Sumo wrestling is an ancient Japanese tradition and the country's official national sport.

Sports

Sumo is Japan's official national sport, in which two large wrestlers grapple to force each other out of a circular area. The martial arts are another Japanese sporting tradition. Japan's **samurai** practised the martial arts judo and jujitsu, which are still popular today. In the martial art Kendo, people use armour and a **bamboo** sword to practise samurai fighting techniques. Karate and aikido are other forms of martial arts from Japan.

Football is a popular sport in Japan, as are tennis and table tennis, basketball, volleyball, swimming, skiing, and snowboarding. Baseball is extremely popular. The best team from each of Japan's two professional baseball leagues plays in the Japan Series each autumn.

Baseball player Daiki Enokida of Japan is pictured here pitching against the Chinese team during the Asian Games, which are held every four years in the region.

Having fun

In their spare time, Japanese children like to play video games. They also enjoy **manga**, which are popular Japanese comic books. **Anime** – Japanese for "animation" – is a popular form of film created from *manga*. Other Japanese films, such as those by director Akira Kurosawa, are internationally famous for their unique artistic qualities.

Karaoke, or "empty orchestra", started in Japan and is still popular. People sing their favourite songs, following lyrics displayed on a screen while the music plays in the background. Other pastimes include origami, which is the art of paper folding. Origami cranes are popular, as the crane is a symbol of good fortune and long life.

Food

Traditional Japanese food is generally healthy. Dishes include rice, seafood, and vegetables. Noodles such as *ramen* and *udon* are also popular. Sashimi is thin slices of raw fish. Sushi is raw fish combined with rice, and sometimes rolled up with seaweed.

Japanese *manga* and *anime* have become popular and influential worldwide.

YOUNG PEOPLE

Young Japanese people who live in cities such as Tokyo are known for their **individuality** and for fashion trends that change very quickly. They like modern music from the **West** such as pop, rock, hip-hop, jazz, and blues. Japanese stars have transformed this music into a form called Japanese pop, or J-pop. Famous female singers such as Hikaru Utada and Ayumi Hamasaki often top the Japanese charts and have influenced the country's popular culture.

Miso soup

Miso soup is a common dish in Japan, and one you will find in Japanese restaurants. Make sure an adult helps you to use the hob in this recipe. You can buy miso paste and dashi soup stock from an Asian market or the international aisle at your supermarket. Keep miso paste in your refrigerator.

Ingredients

20 grams Japanese dashi soup stock
800 millilitres boiling water
200 grams tofu
30 millilitres miso paste
50 grams chopped spring onion

What to do
What to do

1. Put the dashi soup stock and water into a saucepan and bring it to a boil.

2. Cut the tofu into small cubes and add them to the soup.

3. Simmer the tofu in the soup on low heat for four to five minutes.

4. Scoop out some soup stock from the pan into a bowl and dissolve your miso paste into it.

5. Gradually return your miso mixture into the soup, stirring gently (be careful not to boil the soup after this point).

6. Once the mixture is completely stirred in, turn off the heat, and add your chopped spring onion to the soup.

Japan today

Japan has great respect for its history. It has managed to preserve its ancient **culture** even through periods of domination by the **West** and defeat in World War II. In their recovery, the Japanese embraced Western culture and ideas and made them their own. Japan became a peaceful, modern, **industrial** superpower with worldwide influence.

People in cities around the globe seek out sushi or Japanese noodles. They may follow that up with a round of karaoke. It is also likely they will travel in a Japanese car and listen to a Japanese-made stereo along the way. Young people everywhere know Japanese *manga* and *anime*.

New struggles

Japan was already dealing with the worldwide **recession** that had begun in 2008 when major disaster struck in 2011. The Tohoku earthquake of 11 March 2011, and the **tsunami** that followed, devastated Japan. They also damaged the Fukushima nuclear power plant, adding a scary new threat.

Technologies, such as mobile-phone cameras and the Internet, meant that people around the world could watch the horrible disaster unfold. People everywhere came together in support of Japan. With nuclear power providing electricity in many places around the world, people watched and waited to see the impact of what happened at Fukushima.

A strong future

It will take many years to understand the full impact the 2011 natural disasters had on Japan and on the world. The one certainty is the Japanese people's ability to overcome and rebuild. With help from its many international friends, Japan is sure to recover and remain an influential world power.

Japan maintains its traditions while continually reinventing itself.

Fact file

Official name: Japan

Official language: Japanese

Capital city: Tokyo

Population: 126,804,433 (July 2010 est.)

Largest cities (populations): Tokyo (12,989,000)
Yokohama (3,687,382)
Osaka (2,653,552)

System of government: Parliamentary government with a constitutional monarchy

Date of independence: 3 May 1947 (current **constitution** adopted as an amendment to an earlier constitution)

Religions*: **Shintoism** (83.9 per cent), **Buddhism** (71.4 per cent), **Christianity** (2 per cent)
(*Note: Total exceeds 100 per cent because many people follow both Shintoism and Buddhism.)

Life expectancy: 82.17 years

Literacy rate: 99 per cent

Area (total): 364,485 square kilometres (140,728 square miles)

Highest elevation: Fuji-san (Mount Fuji), 3,776 metres (12,388 feet)

Lowest elevation: Hachiro-gata, −4 metres (−13 feet)

These Buddhist monks are praying in front of a temple in Kyoto.

Longest river:	Shinano, 367 kilometres (228 miles)
Largest lake:	Lake Biwa, 670 square kilometres (259 square miles)
Local currency:	Yen
Natural resources:	Negligible mineral resources, fish
Exports:	Transport equipment, motor vehicles, semi-conductors, electrical machinery, chemicals
Imports:	Machinery and equipment, fuels, foodstuffs, chemicals, textiles, raw materials

National bird: Tancho, or red-crowned crane

National flowers: Chrysanthemum (symbol of the **emperor**), plum blossom (represents the first sign of spring), cherry blossom (traditional national flower)

Famous Japanese people:
Ai Sugiyama (born 1975), tennis player
Akio Morita (1921–1999), co-founder of Sony Corporation
Akira Kurosawa (1910–1998), film director
Ayumi Hamasaki (born 1978), singer and songwriter
Hayao Miyazaki (born 1941), **anime** film director
Hideaki Anno (born 1960), *anime* and film director
Ichiro Suzuki (born 1973), baseball player
Minamoto Yoritomo (1147–1199), first **shogun**
Sakichi Toyoda (1867–1930), inventor, founder of
  Toyota Industries
Shikibu Murasaki (*c.* 978–1014), author of world's first novel

National holidays:

1 January	New Year's Day
2nd Monday of January	Coming of Age Day
11 February	National Foundation Day
around 20 March	Spring Equinox Day
29 April	Showa Day
3 May	Constitution Day
4 May	Greenery Day
5 May	Children's Day
3rd Monday of July	Ocean Day
3rd Monday of September	Respect for the Aged Day
around 23 September	Autumn Equinox Day
2nd Monday of October	Health and Sports Day
3 November	Culture Day
23 November	Labour Thanksgiving Day
23 December	Emperor's Birthday

National anthem
"Kimigayo" ("The Emperor's Reign")

*May the reign of the Emperor
continue for a thousand, nay,
eight thousand generations,
the eternity that it takes
for small pebbles to grow into a great rock and become,
covered with moss.*

The **pagoda** building
is a unique Japanese
design.

Timeline

BC is short for "Before Christ". BC is added after a date and means that the date occurred before the birth of Jesus Christ, for example, 450 BC.

AD is short for *Anno Domini*, which is Latin for "in the year of our Lord". AD is added before a date and means that the date occurred after the birth of Jesus Christ, for example, AD 720.

c. 30,000 BC	People begin living in Japan.
c. 10,000 BC	The Jomon **culture** develops.
660 BC	According to legend, the Japanese state is founded by Jimmu, the first **emperor**.
c. 250 BC	A wave of people from mainland Asia, called the Yayoi, come to dominate in Japan. The Yayoi bring farming with them, as well as the working of bronze and iron. They follow a new religion, which eventually develops into **Shintoism**.
AD 500s	The Yamato **clan** founds the **imperial dynasty**, one that has reigned in Japan since this time.
AD 538 or 552	**Buddhism** arrives in Japan from China. Chinese culture has a strong influence on the development of Japan.
1192	Minamoto Yoritomo is appointed **shogun** by Emperor Go-Toba, and the era of the rule of the shoguns in Japan begins.
1543	The Portuguese arrive in Japan, making the first contact between the Japanese and Europeans.
1639	The shoguns close Japan to outside influence and drive out all foreigners.
1707	Mount Fuji's last volcanic eruption occurs.

1853   US Commodore Matthew Perry arrives in Uraga Bay and opens Japan to foreigners and US trade by 1858, using the threat of superior military force.

1868   The era of the shoguns ends, and the emperor is restored to power when Emperor Mutsuhito takes the throne. The Meiji Restoration takes place.

1894   Japan goes to war with China and achieves victory in nine months.

1904   Japan goes to war with Russia and achieves victory in 1905.

1923   An earthquake in the Tokyo region kills around 140,000 people.

1937   Japan goes to war with China and captures Shanghai, Beijing, and Nanjing by the end of the year.

1939   World War II begins in Europe.

1941   Japan launches a devastating surprise attack on 7 December on the US Navy's Pacific Fleet at Pearl Harbor, Hawaii. The United States and the **Allied forces** declare war on Japan the following day.

1945   US planes drop two atomic bombs: one on Hiroshima (6 August) and a second on Nagasaki (9 August). Japan surrenders and is placed under a US military government. All Japanese military and naval forces are disbanded.
World War II ends.

1947   A new **constitution** comes into force, establishing a parliament and allowing all adults to vote. The emperor is granted ceremonial status.

1972   The Japanese prime minister visits China, and normal relations are resumed.

1989   Emperor Hirohito dies and is succeeded by Akihito.

1995   An earthquake hits central Japan, killing thousands and causing massive damage.

1997   The Japanese **economy** enters a severe **recession**.

2009   Economics Minister Kaoru Yosano says Japan is facing its worst economic crisis since World War II.

2011   A huge earthquake and **tsunami** on the east coast kill thousands.

Glossary

acid rain rain that contains harmful acid caused by chemicals in the air

Allied forces countries, including the Great Britain, United States, France, and Russia, that fought against Japan and Germany in World War II

anime Japanese animation

architecture design and style of buildings

bamboo strong, fast-growing plant found in Asia

Buddhism religion originated in India by Buddha (Siddhartha Gautama)

calligraphy beautiful penmanship, especially highly decorative handwriting

Christianity religion based on a belief in the ideas taught by Jesus Christ

clan large family or group of families

Confucianism Chinese way of thought developed by Confucius that teaches loyalty to family and rulers, and to treat others as you would like to be treated

constitution system of laws and principles that govern a nation or state

culture practices, beliefs, and traditions of a society

democracy system in which every citizen of a country can vote to elect government officials

dynasty series of rulers from the same family or group

economy having to do with the money, industries, and jobs in a country

emperor person who rules over an empire, which is a group of countries

environment natural world, including plants and animals

export to ship goods to other countries for sale or exchange

haiku type of Japanese poem with three lines and seventeen syllables

hereditary handed down from one generation of a family to the next

imperial relating to an empire or ruler of an empire

individualism having to do with someone who does things his or her own way, without influence from other people

industrial relating to industry, which involves the large-scale production of goods

industry having to do with large-scale production and business

kimono traditional piece of Japanese clothing similar to a long, loose coat

life expectancy average number of years of life for a group of individuals

manga Japanese comic books

mangrove swamp swamp found in coastal waters and dominated by mangrove trees

pagoda multi-tiered tower, traditionally used as a Buddhist temple

pollution addition of harmful gases or chemicals to the environment, for example, to the air or water

prefecture region of Japan

radiation form of energy in waves that you cannot see. Radiation from nuclear reactions, in large amounts, is harmful to living things.

rainforest tropical forest with dense growth and high annual rainfall

recession difficult economic time when there is less business activity

samurai member of a powerful military class in Japan's past

sanction official order stopping trade with another country in order to force it to make changes

Shintoism ancient, traditional religion of Japan, which includes worship of nature and ancestors

shogun military leader in Japan until the mid-1800s

shrine sacred or holy place

species particular type of animal or plant

sub-tropical related to an area near a tropical region, characterized by warm, humid weather

tsunami very large wave, usually caused by an underwater earthquake, that can cause tremendous damage when it reaches land

typhoon powerful storm that forms over tropical waters in parts of the Pacific Ocean; in other regions, it is called a hurricane or tropical cyclone

West western part of the world, especially Western Europe and North America

Find out more

Books

A World of Recipes: Japan, Julie McCulloch (Heinemann Library, 2009)
Celebrate! Japan, Robyn Hardyman (Franklin Watts, 2009)
Countries in Our World: Japan, Jim Pipe (Franklin Watts, 2010)
Discover Countries: Japan, Susan Crean (Wayland, 2010)
Travel Through Japan, Joe Fullman (QED Publishing, 2007)
Welcome to Japan, Harlinah Whyte and Nicole Frank (Franklin Watts, 2007)

Websites

**https://www.cia.gov/library/publications/the-world-factbook/
index.html**
The World Factbook provides information on the history, people,
government, geography, and more of Japan and over 250 other nations.

web-japan.org/kidsweb/explore/index.html
Learn more about Japan on this website.

whc.unesco.org/en/list
This page on the UNESCO website provides a list of all the World Heritage
sites in Japan and the rest of the world.

**www.prb.org/Datafinder/Geography/Summary.aspx?region=167
&region_type=2**
The website of the Population Reference Bureau provides a lot of data on
Japan's population, education, health, and other statistics.

www.who.int/countries/jpn/en
This website of the World Health Organization (WHO) provides health
information about Japan.

Places to visit

If you are lucky enough to visit Japan, you could visit cities and towns such as Tokyo, Nara, Kyoto, and Osaka. Here are some additional sites to see:

Bomb Dome, Hiroshima
The remains of the Prefectural Industrial Promotion Hall lie under the spot where the atomic bomb "Little Boy" was dropped on Hiroshima on 6 August 1945. Today, it is the centre of the Hiroshima Peace Memorial Park.

Daisetsuzan National Park, Hokkaido
Daisetsuzan is Japan's largest national park and is located in the centre of the northern island of Hokkaido, in rugged mountains.

Himeji Castle, Himeji
Built in the 1300s, Himeji is the most visited castle in Japan.

Kamakura, Kanagawa
The large, outdoor, bronze Buddha is from the 1200s and is over 13.4 metres (43 feet) high.

Matsumoto Castle, Nagano
This is another fine example of a castle from the shogun era in Japan.

Miyajima
Miyajima means "Island of Shrines". The island is especially known for its *torii*, which look as if they are floating. A *torii* is a Japanese gateway that leads to a shrine of the Shinto religion.

Mount Fuji, Chubu
Japan's highest mountain is almost a perfect cone shape and is Japan's best-known landmark.

Topic tools

You can use these topic tools for your school projects. Trace the map on to a sheet of paper, using the black outline to guide you.

The Japanese flag is white, with a large, red disc in the centre. The red disc represents the Sun. The Sun disc has been a symbol in Japan for centuries. The official Japanese name for its flag is *Nisshoki*, meaning "Sun-mark flag". It is more commonly referred to as *Hinomaru*, meaning "Sun disc". The flag was adopted in 1853. Copy the flag design and then colour in your picture. Make sure you use the right colours!

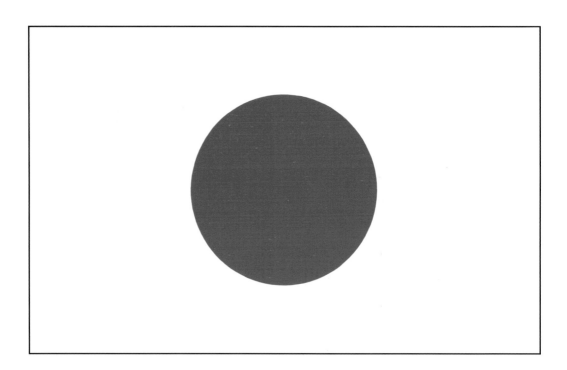

N

Tokyo

Index